Let's Make Love, Then Cook

It's Not What You Think!

Karen Hyles

PROFESSIONAL PUBLISHING MEETS POWERFUL PROMOTION

A wholly owned subsidiary of **T B N**

Let's Make Love, Then Cook

Trilogy Christian Publishers A Wholly Owned Subsidiary of Trinity Broadcasting Network

2442 Michelle Drive Tustin, CA 92780

For information about special discounts for bulk purchases, please contact Trilogy Christian Publishing.

Trilogy Disclaimer: The views and content expressed in this book are those of the author and may not necessarily reflect the views and doctrine of Trilogy Christian Publishing or the Trinity Broadcasting Network.

Manufactured in the United States of America

10 9 8 7 6 5 4 3 2 1

Library of Congress Cataloging-in-Publication Data is available.

ISBN: 978-1-68556-153-6

E-ISBN: 978-1-68556-154-3

Dedication

This book is dedicated to the millennial and Z generations or younger disciples and younger pastors and preachers. After following Jesus for thirty years plus, I wanted to pass on a few words of wisdom and what I've learned from Him to you. I wanted to use my words to encourage you, should you find yourself going through "hard times."

I also wanted to say: Finally, I've finished. I got it all out, everything I wanted to say to seven generations of grandchildren who are coming behind me so the "family name" will be blessed forever.

Acknowledgments

I want to thank *senior* pastors everywhere. If you are a senior pastor, I want to thank you for your sacrifice, for the nights you prayed for your church members. For all the preaching and teaching you did, as you tried your best to help us follow Jesus Christ and have a personal relationship with Him. And for the stress that you endured trying to provide or rent a church building, buy airtime on television and radio, and publish books, etc.

So that we can have access to the Word of God and God's love, I want to thank you, senior pastors, for carrying the church on your shoulders for all these years. I'm so grateful for your service. I do not have words to express; my heart is so full. Tears are running down my face as I write this. Your words saved my life, pastors. What I'm trying to say is that God used you to bring me home to Him.

For years, I sat there in the church building, listening to all your sermons and preaching messages, quietly allowing the Holy Spirit to use your words to change me. And I said to myself, one day, I will make you proud, pastors. I want you to know that your labor of love was not in vain. I want to thank you all for being my "spiritual parents." I love you, senior pastors.

Acknowledgments

Table of Contents

Introduction

I have no fancy college degree, and I have nothing special going on. I'm not a pastor. All I have is the Holy Spirit. If you wish to be discipleship and need answers, this book is for you.

Before we begin, all *Scripture verses* are from the NKJV.

Talking about *growth*... Let's play pretend and, if I may, represent the senior pastors. If I keep standing in front of you and praying for you, you won't grow; therefore, I have to step aside. I can't "baby" these kids or church members, or they'll never grow in their prayer life.

Groups and group discussions are great for connecting, but we're so busy preaching to the group that the "individual" is suffering.

Growth or discipleship, on the other hand, is all about that one on one, quality time spent investing and helping you discover learning about yourself and God, who you are, and who He is; character building.

At some point, the individual or church members have to learn to pray and believe God for themselves. So how do you "wean" the kids off other people praying for them? And stop treating them like baby Christians because they can't remain babies forever.

If we learned one thing from the 2020 pandemic, it is that we weren't ready. Senior pastors hadn't trained their church members to pray for themselves. I saw the panic in the eyes of the "baby" church members as they were running everywhere trying to get someone to pray for them. God forbid if there's another pandemic in the future. But like Bishop T. D. Jakes says, "This time, I'll be ready." I want to be ready and not caught off guard. So, how did I learn to pray for myself?

Answer: When I was a baby Christian, I called the church phone number in hopes that a pastor would pray for me. And I could not get a hold of anyone. At first, I was so angry that my needs weren't being met. But I soon realized that this was an opportunity for me to grow and learn how to pray for myself.

And I also had tough love. "Open the Bible," they said. "Say what the Word of God says about you. Are you feeling anxious? What does the Bible say about it?" they told me. And that's how I quickly learned how to pray.

Things I want apprentices or disciples to know is that if everyone prayed for you and you listened to all the preaching and teaching in the world and read all the books, at some point, you would still have to do it for yourself, grow. You won't grow if I keep giving you all the answers. At some point, you have to get the answers for yourself. Get your own answers from God. Get your own stories! I could inspire you with my stories, and you would say it's amazing, but it's your turn now, young preachers, pastors, church members, to get your "own" stories and answers.

Always remember, the first person you lead is you...

Anyway, *Let's Make Love, Then Cook* is about prayer, talking to God, worship, and learning how to cook or prepare to preach, teach, being used by God, serving Him.

I will walk through the sixty-six books in the Bible to find direct conversations between God and mankind. And I found plenty.

Books have been written about prayer, but people still struggle to pray. So, I decided to write about examples of Bible characters praying or talking to God about everything and serving Him. This is what the pastors mean when they say to pray or talk to God.

Continued Growth

The hardest thing about being a child is having to let go

of Mom and Dad and walk on your own. The Bible says, "When I was a child…but when I became a man, I put away childish things" (1 Corinthians 13:11, NKJV).

And of course, the hardest thing about being a parent is having to stop, no more suggestions or giving advice. You have to let the child make his or her own decisions, and you have to respect them. The child has to decide whether they will continue to let the parent "baby" them or "grow up, mature, take responsibility" for their life. Have you noticed God seemed to stop speaking in this pandemic? As if to say, the teacher is always silent when the student is taking an "open book" test. You know the answers already; you've heard it preached for years. The answers to life's problems or your circumstances are in your Bible.

Jesus spent three and a half years pouring into His disciples (John 16:5–15), and then He stepped aside so that they could grow.

I encourage you to do what He did, become like Him, a "mini-me" version of Him, running around on the planet, loving people.

Let's Make Love, Then Cook is also about drawing near to God, for He will draw near to you (James 4:8).

It is a book about spending time in prayer and relationship with God and ministry or service to Him.

Who wants to read another book about prayer and ministry? It sounds so boring.

I wanted to make it interesting! I thought I would *jass* it up a little, make it something that you would want to read about.

Instead of teaching and preaching about prayer or being in a relationship with God, I wanted to give examples from the Bible or show you mankind talking to God.

I also wanted to show that we preach, teach the Bible, write books about the Bible, and get together in our groups to talk about prayer, but we do know how to get alone with God and pray for ourselves.

This book will explore several relationships in the Bible and their conversations with God and show you how they prayed or talked with Him.

I want to encourage you to develop your "own" relationship with Him and let Him "use" you.

Body

Here Are Examples of How to Pray:

Prayer, talking to God, and my relationship with Him.

Chapter 1

Karen's Story

This is about building my relationship with Jesus and drama! Yes, child, juicy, isn't it? As if made for a soap opera! Would you like me to give you the details, my friend? Here it goes!

I'd like to start off by telling you about my relationship with Jesus Christ.

I'd always heard about Him through third parties or preachers, but I had never been officially introduced. One day, He got my attention through Pastor Frederick K. C. Price's television ministry and extended His right hand of fellowship for relationship and connection.

"Hi," I said, "who are you?"

"Jesus," He said.

"I heard through third parties that you can save me," I said.

"Yes, pray with Me," He said.

"Wow, how cool is that?" I asked. "I want to get to

know you better."

"Follow Me, go on this journey with Me," He said.

"Great," I said.

Nice guy, I thought, talking about Jesus. *Not trying to exploit me; this is different. I'm still keeping one eye open, though; just in case, smile!*

"Where are we going?" I asked.

"To church," Jesus said.

"Why?" I asked.

"To meet the rest of My family or body of Christ," He said.

"So soon? I'm not properly dressed," I said.

"Don't worry; you can come as you are. Welcome to the body of Christ," He said.

"What's happening to me?" I asked.

"You're experiencing baptism in water. I got you; you won't drown," Jesus said.

"I feel clean, like the old me is dead and the new me is raised from the dead with Christ," I said.

"How do you like the journey so far?" He asked.

Chapter 1

"Strange, but good," I said. "Where to now?" I asked.

"We're going to receive the baptism of the Holy Spirit with the evidence of speaking with other tongues (Acts 1:8; Acts 2:4)," He said.

"Oh, more baptism," I said.

"You're getting the royal makeover: facial, pedicure, the whole nine yards, two for one deal, the works, baby girl. Trust Me, you're going to look and feel different when this is all over," Jesus said.

"If You say so, I trust You," I said.

I never had a man take care of me like this before; this was all new to me. *So far, so good*, I thought.

"Pack your bags," Jesus said.

"Pack my bags, leave family, friends, loved ones, and go into the unknown? What's out there? Is it safe?" I asked.

"Walk by faith, and I will never leave you nor forsake you," He said. "I will protect you, according to Psalm 91."

"What about food?" I asked.

"I will provide for you, according to Philippians 4:19," He said.

Listen to Him. First, He protects me, then provides for

me. What's next? I hope He's not planning on putting a ring on it. He might be one of those fast talkers or a smooth operator, too good to be true. I'm gonna play hard to get; I'm not that easy. I'm still keeping one eye open, though; You don't fool me, I said to myself.

"Why are we stopping here?" I asked.

"We need gas money," He said.

I had packed a bag of clothes and, with eighty dollars in my hand, headed onto the I-5 north freeway, from California to Seattle, Washington. But I ran out of gas when I got to the Tacoma Dome. Pastor Benny Hinn was doing a healing crusade, so I went inside.

Less than five minutes into the worship service, someone tapped me on the shoulder and said, "Don't forget to read Isaiah 61."

"Okay," I said.

But they did it again, tapped me on the shoulder, and said, "Don't forget to read Isaiah 61."

"Thank you," I said.

But they said it a third time, "Don't forget to read Isaiah 61."

"Hmm," I said.

Chapter 1

They must have really wanted me to read this Bible verse, so I opened my Bible and turned to Isaiah 61, and I was about to read it when I saw the money. Lo and behold, there were 71 dollars in my Bible. *How did that get there?* I thought. It was more than enough for gas. I turned around to thank the people that tapped me on the shoulder, but they were gone. People or angels, I don't know. All I knew was He provided like He said He would.

I was beginning to see that He might be a man of His word. He keeps His promises. I was impressed but still keeping one eye open. Not going to win me over that easily, work for my love, my friend!

"I want you to register for Bible college," He said.

"Me? What do I know about being in the ministry?" I asked.

"You know nothing, but I'm going to use these Bible teachers to train you," Jesus said.

We made it to the city of Federal Way, Seattle, and He said to me, "Get a job; you need a place to stay. Tomorrow, we will register for Bible college."

I grabbed a newspaper and found one of those live-in caretaker positions and told them I had no experience, but they hired me anyway. God provided again.

The next morning, off we went to register for Bible college at Dominion College, run by Pastor Casey Treat.

"Who do You want me to be when I grow up?" I asked because I was twenty-two years old at the time.

And Jesus said to me, "I want to see you as a mother of nations. I want to see My children healed, healthy, and whole," He said.

I was lying in my bed one night at about 3 a.m. when He said it three times to me, *as a mother of nations...*

Wow, I have my own little purpose in life, I thought.

"Talk to Me," He said.

I never liked talking. My parents said that I was to be seen but not heard. So, I sat there in deep thought, thinking and thinking and feeling depressed.

"Talk to Me," He said again.

I kept sitting there, thinking and feeling depressed. I had learned to keep it all in, so I sat there, thinking and thinking.

"Talk to Me," He said again.

Finally, I snapped.

"What do you want me to say? I don't know how to

talk; I'm not the queen of gab, I'm not an extrovert, You know?" I said to Jesus.

"This is good. Start there, tell Me all about it," He said. "I want to be your wonderful counselor," He said.

Before I knew it, words were falling out of my mouth. I told Him everything.

"Guess what I did at work today?" I asked. "I'm going to the market; want to come?" I asked.

Before long, He became my BFF (best friend forever).

"Good afternoon, Jesus, I'm home," I would say. I treated Him like a person.

Before long, He became my High Priest. I went to Him to confess my sins.

"Jesus," I said.

"Yes, Karen?" He said.

"It just dawned on me that I'm a sinner; I need Your forgiveness," I said.

"I forgive you," He said.

"Just like that? Too easy," I said.

"Simply believe," He said.

I was gullible, naïve. So, I decided to simply believe like a little child. I remember Him saying something about little children who inherited the kingdom.

"I believe. I'm forgiven," I said. "Woo-hoo!"

"Karen, I want you to become like Me," said Jesus.

"What are You saying? Do You not like the way I am? You want me to change?" I asked. "I knew it. There it was, Catch-22," I said. *I can't get something for nothing. I have to give Him something. I have to give Him me*, I thought.

"Die to self, pick up my cross; that's what You're saying, right?" I asked.

"Right, become like Me, more loving, etc.," Jesus said.

"I see. I have to think about this," I said. Because this meant that I would have to change my nature, behavior, attitude, and renew my mind, according to Romans 12:2.

"It will be hard, but you can do all things through Christ who strengthens you (Philippians 4:13)," He said.

English as a Second Language

I had to learn to speak American. Speak American! Yes, that's right, it's a thing!

I could speak English, but coming from a third-world

country, I spoke broken English. It was a mixture of Caribbean and British languages.

The year was 1985 or 1987 when I came to America. I was fifteen years old at the time. It was a culture shock and such a contrast. I was used to the farmers market, and if they were out of that product, they were out. Everything was fresh. Because it came from somebody's farm or backyard, you had to wait until the next day to get your items. The contrast was that in America, they have grocery stores. It was shocking to me! I couldn't believe it. There was no running out of food! What a mind-bender!

I remembered one day, my mom took me to the store, and I started grabbing milk. I thought they were going to run out of supplies. So, I grabbed everything, 1 percent, 2 percent, 3 percent! Is there a three percent? I don't know. All I know is, I grabbed all kinds of milk—chocolate milk, strawberry milk, almond milk, goat milk. Well! You just never know! Finally, my mom did her best to calm me down. "It's here all days; there's more in the back; we won't run out," she said.

I was born in South America, Guyana, on January 20th, 1972. Weighing at six pounds, seven ounces, I made my way into this place called earth. The crazy nurse slapped me to make sure that I was breathing and to get me to let out my baby cry. So, at the top of my lungs, I decreed with my little, tiny voice, "I'm here. I've arrived!"

And so, I began my trek through this planet. The crazy nurse again wanted to put me in an orphanage or a foster home because my mom was sick with TB (tuberculosis) at the time of my birth and couldn't take care of me.

So, the crazy nurse thought it was a good idea to put me with a bunch of strangers. Some nerve! That nurse, somebody ought to have slapped her! The devil is a liar; I wasn't going anywhere.

The next thing I knew, my grandmother stuffed me in her pocket and ran out of the hospital with me. True story! She actually did it! Well, you go, Granny! Needless to say, I did end up on the milk carton box as a missing person. See, I told you, I was staying with family, not strangers.

The Sugar Plantation or Life In…

I want to tell you how I developed my sweet tooth and my life in Guyana. I put sugar on everything. If you could eat it, I put sugar on it. Sugar on top of ice cream, my friends. Yummy! It reminds me of the Christmas movie called *Elf*. There's a scene where the actor, Will Ferrell, playing Elf, puts syrup on his spaghetti dinner. That's me, my friends. If I'm going to die, I might as well die happy.

Chapter 1

Smile! Right! For real!

I mostly enjoyed my life in Guyana. I spent most of my childhood and some of my teenage years there. Sugar was first grown in colonial Guyana in 1658 but was not produced on a large scale until the late 1700s. To require the labor for sugar cultivation, plantations at first imported slaves from West Africa. Anyway…

From birth to five years old, I lived with my grandmother, feeling loved. But then, my grandmother came to America.

From five to nine years old, I lived with my parents. Life was hard. There was lots of verbal and physical abuse; they told me that I would never amount to anything. But God had a plan, according to Jeremiah 29:11. And then, my parents came to America.

From nine to fifteen years old, I lived with my aunts. Life wasn't too bad. I got to play, be a child. I remembered this one childhood game we used to play. It's called "catch me," if I remember correctly, my brain is getting a little foggy. Anyway, the rule of the game was your feet could not touch the ground. If your feet touched the ground, it meant you were out of the game. We had to swing from tree limb to tree limb without our feet touching the ground. Fun times, my friends. Upper body strength was a must-have in this game. So I became a tomboy. You had to be strong to play and keep playing in this game. The best part of the game, though, was hanging in the tree, eating all kinds of fruit—mangoes, bananas, watermelon, etc. And when we were thirsty, we drank coconut water and ate the jelly. And when we wanted something sweet to eat, we ate the sugar cane! It was natural raw sugar. That was the best part of my childhood.

From fifteen to twenty-one years old, I started my life in America. Here, I had to learn English as a second language and find a way to fit in. I had to learn to speak American. Today, if you hear me speak, if you listen really hard, you might hear an accent. I tried hard not to use broken English, but…

I remember this one time I had to write on a piece of paper what I wanted my food order to be because the teachers and students at my high school couldn't understand what I was trying to say. Right there, I knew I had to try really hard to fit in.

High school was so difficult because, in my country, the high school kids graduated at age fourteen. I thought I was off to college. Imagine how I felt coming to America only to hear I had another four years of high school to go.

Eight years of high school, are you kidding me? Seriously! Good night! (Good night means "for crying out loud.") Anyway, I survived by the grace of God.

From twenty-two years old to current, I have been "adulting" and giving my heart to Christ Jesus and in service to Him.

I struggled with my relationships, making the right choices, good judgment, and my career path. I felt like a loser and failure to launch. But what I didn't know at the time was that this crushing feeling would lead me to Him... Jesus.

It was meant for evil, to discourage me. There I was, a young person without a plan and no prospects. But God! I learned something that day: all things work together for good for those who are called, according to His purpose (Romans 8:28).

2020 Pandemic and Getting Through It

There I was, struggling to understand what was happening to me in this pandemic; you know, English as a second language all over again. I was trying to make sense of this pandemic. Was it man-made or natural? Hmm! Was I sick for real, or did I think myself into the symptoms of feeling sick? Hmm! And, will the vaccine save me or kill me? Hmm! And, who should I listen to? Everything and everyone was polarized. What was I to do?

The world was changing so fast. Today, they say it's blue. Tomorrow, they tell me that it's changed, it's now yellow. I found myself moving from job site to job site, trying to stay ahead of COVID-19. I was scared to death but determined not to show it. "Control your emotions and mind, Karen," I said to myself. "You're too legit to quit," I said. "Let everybody know that this is what we mean when we say Christian or fearless."

This 2020 pandemic came to reveal who I really was. Was I a scared little Christian? Or was I like the Christians in the Bible, an overcomer? Thanks to this pandemic, though, I found out who I really am. I am somebody's child, and "my Father" God loves me so much.

Chapter 2

First, let's define what a relationship is. A relationship is a way two people talk to each other or connect. Some examples of relationships are family, friendships, work, romantic, and teacher/student relationships. But I'm not focusing on those relationships. What I want to focus on is the relationship between God and His creation, mankind. Let's see what the Bible has to say about relationships.

In 1 Corinthians 13:1–13, it talks about how we are to treat each other. And Galatians 5:1–16 talks about the fruit or characteristics that we should bear.

Prayer, Talking to God, and Relationship with Him #1

Let's begin by looking at this relationship between God and mankind. According to Genesis 1:26–30 and Genesis 2:4–7, God created man.

"Then the Lord God called to Adam and said to him, 'Where are you?' So he said, 'I heard your voice in the garden, and I was afraid because I was naked; and I hid myself'" (Genesis 3:9–10).

Now, this is the first time we see God and mankind

talking and connecting. What I like about this is that they were talking. Father God and Adam, His "created" son, were having a Father/son conversation.

"My son, where are you?" says Father God. "I just want to talk, hang out, you know? We boys, right? Where you at, son? I miss talking with you." It is as if I can hear the earnestness in His voice. "Come now, and let us reason together" (Isaiah 1:18), He said.

Can you hear Him today calling you? When I listened to my Father God, it sounded like, "Karen, let's have a tea party with the teacups in the dollhouse, and let's play dress up."

Ladies, you know what I'm talking about. Remember when you were young and played or wanted to play? It's the same thing here. "I'm coming, Daddy; this is our little special date or 'prayer time,'" I said.

Prayer, Talking to God, and Relationship with Him #2

Here's another relationship of man talking to God or praying. Now, in this story, Cain decides to kill his brother Abel because the Lord God respected Abel's offering and not his (Genesis 4:1–15).

> Then, the Lord said to Cain, "Where is your brother?" And He said, "I do not know. Am I my

32

brother's keeper? And the Lord said, "What have you done? The voice of your brother's blood cries out to Me from the ground, so now you are cursed from the earth, which has opened its blood and received your brother's blood from your hand. When you till the ground, it shall no longer yield its strength to you. A fugitive and a vagabond you shall be on the earth."

And Cain said to the Lord, "My punishment is greater than I can bear! Surely You have driven me out from the face of the ground; I shall be hidden from Your face, I shall be a fugitive and a vagabond and the earth, and it will happen that anyone who finds me will kill me." And the Lord said to Cain, "Therefore, whoever kills Cain, vengeance shall be taken on him sevenfold." And the Lord set a mark on Cain, lest anyone finding him should kill him.

Genesis 4:9–15 (NKJV)

I wondered why he didn't just ask the Lord to forgive him! "Just own it, brother." It's not blame but responsibility. The Lord already knows what you did anyway! Why hide it? You might as well go ahead and admit that you were wrong for being "jealous" of your brother's offering, killing him for it, and not being the older brother who protected his younger brother, being his keeper.

The Bible says we've all sinned and fallen short of the glory of God, so you're in good company, bro! No one here is judging you, but there have to be some consequences for your actions.

Prayer, talking to God, and Relationship with Him #3

"After these things, the Word of the Lord came to Abram in a vision, saying, "Do not be afraid, Abram, I am your shield, your exceedingly great reward." But Abram said, "Lord God, what will you give me seeing I go childless" (Genesis 15:1–2, NKJV). "Ask, and you shall receive" (John 16:24, NKJV). Hmm! What will you give me, if I ask? I wondered.

Prayer, talking to God, and Relationship with Him #4

Genesis 18:16–33, Abraham intercedes for Sodom.

"And the Lord said, 'Shall I hide from Abraham what I am doing'" (Genesis 18:16). "Then the men turned away from there and went towards Sodom, but Abraham stood still before the Lord. And Abraham came near and said, 'Would You also destroy the righteous with the wicked?'" (Genesis 18:22–23).

I, too, will pray without ceasing (1 Thessalonians 5:17; Romans 8:26–27).

Chapter 2

Prayer, talking to God, and Relationship with Him #5

I must sacrifice what I love (Genesis 22:1–19).

> Now it came to pass after these things that God
> tested Abraham, and said to him, "Abraham!"
> And he said, "Here I am." Then He said, "Take
> now your son, your only son Isaac, whom you
> love, and go to the land of Moriah, and offer him
> there as a burnt offering on one of the mountains
> of which I shall tell you."

Genesis 22:1–2 (NKJV)

There is nothing painful like having to sacrifice what
you love, like my son, my man, and my social media ministry. Don't ask me to give this up! These are my favorites!
You can have the junk, but these are my best toys! "No,
I'm not giving it up or away," I said to the Lord. But what
I didn't understand was that God wanted to see who I worship more, God or mammon. God or money! God or my
relationships! God or my stuff, etc. Hands trembling, I laid
what I loved or wanted to keep for myself on the altar only
to hear, "This is a test," by the emergency broadcasting network. This was only a test! Say what! Whew! Sweat off my
brow! I thought it was for real! The Bible says, "Thou shall
have no other gods before Me" (Exodus 20:3, NKJV). It
also says, "You shall worship the Lord your God, and Him
only shall thou serve" (Luke 4:8, NKJV).

Man! I wouldn't wish this on my worst enemy; it was so stressful. I'm grateful that I went through it, but I never want to do this again. Spare me the drama! For real! Okay?

Prayer, talking to God, and Relationship with Him #6

Exodus 3:1–22; Exodus 4:1–17

> Then Moses said to the Lord, "O my Lord, I am not eloquent, neither before or since You have spoken to your servant; but I am slow of speech and slow of tongue." So the Lord said to Him, "who has made man's mouth? Or who made the mute, the deaf, the seeing or the blind? Have not I, the Lord? "Now therefore, go and I will be with your mouth and teach you what to say."
>
> Exodus 4:10–12 (NKJV)

And all throughout the books of Exodus, Leviticus, Numbers, the Lord spoke to Moses.

"I'm an introvert, really shy and tongue-tied," I said to the Lord. "Why don't You ask the queen of gab to do it? You know, some outgoing extrovert, not this socially challenged person," I said. But unlike Moses, I never asked for a spokesperson. I figured God equips the call or this person. So, I said to the Lord, "If You're going to use me, use me with my cracks and all, insecurities and all." And He nodded.

"We have an understanding then," the Lord said.

Prayer, talking to God, and Relationship with Him #7

He will talk to you about your death (Deuteronomy 31:14–16; Deuteronomy 32:48–52).

"Then the Lord said to Moses, 'Behold, the days approach when you must die; call Joshua...'" (Deuteronomy 31:14, NKJV).

To be "absent" from this "body" is to be "present" with the "Lord" (2 Corinthians 5:1–8). We all have to go at some point. I'm just grateful that I made "my reservations" ahead of time, you know? Like repented of my sins before God and gave my heart to Jesus Christ, according to Romans 10:9–13.

Prayer, talking to God, and Relationship with Him #8

The Lord spoke to Joshua too (Joshua 1:1–9; Joshua 3:7–8).

> "Moses, My servant is dead. Now therefore, arise... Be strong and be very courageous... This Book of the Law shall not depart from your mouth... For the Lord your God is with you wherever you go."
>
> And the Lord said to Joshua, "This day I will be-

gin to exalt you in the sight of all Israel, that they may know that, as I was with Moses, so I will be with you."

Joshua 1:2, 6, 8, 9; 3:7 (NKJV)

"With me, this is good," I said to the Lord.

Promotion cometh from the Lord (Psalm 75:6–8).

God will prepare you for transition and leadership roles and responsibilities.

Prayer, talking to God, and Relationship with Him #9

"Cause the sun to stand still, so that I may kick them," prayed Joshua. Wow, that's a bad boy, praying a prayer like that. He must really know his God. "You go, Joshua." If I had to interview Joshua, I would ask this question: "What happened, bro? Why would you pray a prayer like that?"

I could just hear Joshua say, "These crazy people had the nerve to approach the people of God or Israel. Five kings were attacking one king, so I had to help out."

"I'd like to help out too. Go ahead, enlist me in the Lord's army; you feel me!"

"I have a knuckle sandwich for somebody."

"You're speaking my language, bro," I would say to

Joshua.

Prayer, talking to God, and Relationship with Him #10

Samuel hears God for the first time (1 Samuel 3:1–21).

I remembered when I heard God calling me.

Ring! Ring!

"What gives, woman, don't you hear me calling you?" Jesus asked.

"That was You," I said. "How am I supposed to recognize Your voice?" I asked. "I mean, You're invisible, and You speak in tongues (Acts 2:4)," I said, "plus, Your ways are higher than my ways" (Isaiah 55:8–9). "How was I to make out what You were saying?" I asked.

"Feisty, this one, I like it, she talks back to me," He said.

It took years before I understood His dialect. So, how did I discern it was Him? Answer: years of reading the Bible. God never contradicts His Word. What He whispered in my heart are the very words that He spoke or wrote in the Bible. It would take trial by error, and a few missed turns before I slowly but surely started putting two and two together that the still small voice that I hear in my heart was and still is Him.

Prayer, talking to God, and Relationship with Him #11

Judges 6:11–40; Judges 7:1–25

> Then the Lord turned to Gideon and said, "Go in this might of yours, and you shall save Israel…"
>
> So Gideon said, "How can I save Israel? Indeed my clan is the weakness in Manasseh, and I am the least in my father's house."
>
> And the Lord said to Him, "Surely I will be with you…" Then the Lord said to Gideon, "By the three hundred who lapped I will save you, and deliver the Midianites into your hand."

Judges 6:14–16, 7:7 (NKJV)

Don't feel bad, Gideon; my parents told me for years that I was the weak link. But what I like about God is that He tends to use the foolish things of the earth to confound the wise (1 Corinthians 1:26–31). That's right, Gideon, I will call you Hercules, Hercules!

Prayer, talking to God, and Relationship with Him #12

1 Kings 3:5–15

> At Gibeon, the Lord appeared to Solomon in a dream by night, and God said, "Ask! What shall I give you?"

And Solomon said: "...Now, O Lord, my God, You have made Your servant king instead of my father David, but I am a little child... Therefore give to Your servant an understanding heart to judge Your people that I will discern between good and evil."

The speech pleased the Lord, that Solomon asked Him this thing. Then God said to him: "Because you didn't ask for long life, or riches for yourself nor the life of your enemies... see I have given you a "wise" and understanding heart..."

1 Kings 3:5–7, 9–12 (NKJV)

Prayer, talking to God, and Relationship with Him #13

Job 38:1–41; Job 39:1–30; Job 40:1–24; Job 41:1–34; Job 42:1–17

Then the Lord answered Job out of the whirlwind and said, "I will question you, and you shall answer Me. "Where were you when I laid the foundations of the earth? Tell me..." (Job 38:3–4, NKJV).

If there's one thing I learned in the presence of the Lord, it is when to be quiet and take notes. God is speaking, my friends, don't interrupt Him. Remember what happened to Simon Peter (Luke 9:28–36).

Jesus was talking to Moses, and Elijah and Peter jumped into the conversation. So God finally said, "This is my beloved Son, hear Him!" In other words, shut up and listen. It would be wise, my friends, to listen. You don't want to be rebuked by God.

Prayer, talking to God, and Relationship with Him #14

Throughout the Gospel of Matthew, Mark, Luke, and John, we see Jesus speaking with His disciples.

> Now it came to pass, as He was praying in a certain place, when He ceased, that one of His disciples to Him, "Lord, teach us to pray, as John taught his disciples." So He said to them, "When you pray, say: 'Our Father in heaven, Hallowed be Your name. Your kingdom come. Your will be done on earth as it is in heaven. Give us day by day our daily bread. And forgive our sins, for we also forgive everyone who is indebted to us. And do not lead us into temptation, but deliver us from the evil one.'"

Luke 11:1–4 (NKJV)

So Holy Spirit, please teach me how to pray. The key, my friends, is to ask for help. When you don't know what to say, the Holy Spirit will make intercession (Romans 8:26).

Chapter 2

Prayer, talking to God, and Relationship with Him #15

Acts 9:1–19

> As he journeyed, he came near Damascus, and suddenly a light shone around him from heaven. Then he fell to the ground, and heard a voice saying to him, "Saul, Saul, why are you persecuting Me?" And he said, "Who are you, Lord?" Then the Lord said, "I am Jesus, whom you are persecuting. It is hard for you to kick against the goads." So he, trembling and astonished, said, "Lord, what do You want me to do?" Then the Lord said to Him, "Arise, and go into the city and you will be told what to do."

Acts 9:3–6 (NKJV)

Final Word, Prayer, Talking with God...

Whether He speaks to you in a dream, visions, or you receive a word of the Lord, as He did with the prophet Jeremiah, or an angel of the Lord talked to you like they did with Hagar, Deborah, Mary, etc., and should He speak to you in direct conversations, as He did with Adam, Cain, Abraham, Moses, etc., God wants to speak with you too.

Chapter 3: Worship

When you're irritated, take a spiritual bath.

Don't just sing songs, give lip service, go through the motions. The Bible says, "These people...honor Me with their lips, but their heart is far from Me" (Matthew 15:8, NKJV).

"Love the Lord your God with all of your heart, soul, mind, and strength" (Matthew 12:30, NKJV).

In other words, with everything, don't hold back. When you're tired, irritated, and frustrated, take a spiritual bath, climb into the pond or pool of praise and worship. Don't wait or just worship on Sunday or Wednesday, but whenever you feel stress, anxiety, depression, anger, etc. Watch how quickly your mood starts to change. I noticed that I felt more empowered, more refreshed, and more joyful when I did that. Like I can take on Goliath or "big problems" with a toothpick, know what I mean? that strong. Like an overcomer! King David was all about worship; read the Book of Psalms. He wrote a psalm, or song, about everything. If he was angry, he sang about it to the Lord, and if he was sad or happy, he sang about it to the Lord.

Chapter 4: In Preparation for Ministry

How to Make the Anointed Oil

Exodus 30:22–33 describes how they made the anointing oil back in the day. But in today's world, let's look at how the "oil" was "made" in my life. Yes, pastors prayed for me to be anointed with the laying on of hands.

But what I'm talking about is what I had to go through to develop and make "this particular anointing oil." Enough said! Let's get onto the making of my special oil.

First, liquid myrrh needed to be added, then sweet-smelling cinnamon, sweet-smelling cane, cassia, and a hint of olive oil.

So! Should you find yourself experiencing a "bitter-sweet" moment, just remember myrrh, cinnamon, cane, and cassia is being added to anoint you. And should you find yourself "feeling crushed," I want you to consider that olive oil has just been added to make your anointing oil. This, my friends, is how you prepare for the ministry.

After that, I went on to do all types of ministry. Prison ministry, sing in the choir, group, host, greet, social media ministry—like Facebook and Churchome app—now books, etc. Thirty-plus years later, we're still walking and talking to each other, and God is still using me.

Loving Him and loving His people has been the highlight of my life.

Chapter 5: So Let's Get on with the Cooking: Time to Create the Fancy Feast

---

The Ingredients

I always seem to have food and cooking on my mind, so I thought I would use cooking as a metaphor when it comes to preparing for the ministry, preaching, or teaching.

The first thing you need to know is that we must gather and add the ingredients.

Ingredients #1

Like Pastor Judah Smith (Pastor J) always says, "Look for Jesus" whenever you read the Bible. Whether you read the Old or New Testament, it is all about Him. The Bible is all about Jesus.

Ingredients #2

Ask the Holy Spirit, "How would You have me answer

this question in the Bible?" For example, "What's going on in this verse, paragraph, or one of these sixty-six books?"

Ingredients #3

Speak faith over the Bible message that you prepare. For example, I have faith in God, that while I am preaching or teaching, the eyes of their understanding will be open (Ephesians 1:18). I have faith in God that after I'm done preaching, people will come forward to receive the gift of forgiveness and follow Jesus.

Ingredients #4

Anoint your Bible message before you preach or teach. For example, "Lord Jesus, I ask that you anoint my message and use it for your glory."

Ingredients #5

Praise and worship God for your message *before* you preach or teach. Give back to the Lord. Thank Him for giving to you. Remember, you didn't come up with this message on your own. It was given to you by the inspiration of the Holy Spirit.

Ingredients #6

Last but not least, you gotta remember to give 'em blood. This means being transparent, vulnerable, real, sharing a little bit of yourself, telling us what God did for you and how you got through it, your pain, your struggles, etc.

Now that you have assembled ingredients together: go ahead and start cooking or preaching.

Chapter 6: Examples of My Fancy Feast or Cooking

Fancy Feast #1

Welcome to planet earth! How do you like your stay so far or journey through life?

If you need any help, please see customer service or the B.I.B.L.E., better known as "Basic Instructions Before Leaving Earth."

Fancy Feast #2

Are you trying to solve the puzzle of your life? Have you searched everywhere and still can't find the missing piece? God's love is what's missing! (John 3:16)

Fancy Feast #3

Because He's your nosy neighbor, have you noticed He's always listening in on your conversations? Sometimes I am tempted to say, "Mind your own business, bruh! All up in my business!"

"Anyway, thank You, Jesus, for being my nosy neighbor." "Because where two or three are gathered in My name, I am there in the midst of them" (Matthew 18:20, NKJV).

Fancy Feast #4

Let me introduce you to the Wonder Woman of the Bible! Supergirl ain't got nothing on me! Ladies, when you walk with God, you too can become superwomen. "Certainly I will go with you, but because of the course you are taking, the honor will not be yours, for the Lord will deliver Sisera into the hands of a woman," says Deborah (Judges 4:9, NKJV).

She said, "I just want you to know that your behind got beat by a woman today!" Wow! That's a bad woman right there, not messing with you, girl; just grateful you're on my team!

Fancy Feast # 5

Help me become Batman! Like Batman, I had to face my fear. Batman had to face his fears of bats. But I had to face my fear of belonging, believing, and becoming like Jesus. It's true, you know, "I can do all things through Christ who strengthens me" (Philippians 4:13, NKJV). And you can too!

Fancy Feast # 6

The Miranda rights... Busted! I have a warrant for your arrest! You have not been following Jesus. I'm going to have to book you and take you in! You have the right to keep committing a sin or start praying and praising God. Your bail is set on being free and being delivered from sin. Anything you've done, if you confess, will be forgiven, and you will be saved, according to Romans 10:9–13. "I am the *cop* who busted you because I love you," says Jesus.

Chapter 7: Questions and Answers Forum

There are questions that were asked on the Churchome app. I thought my *answers* might *help* somehow.

The *key*, or another *secret*, is to treat the questions and answer forum like a Nintendo game. Every question you answer takes you to a whole other level or "understanding of God and yourself." First things first, listen to Daily Guided Prayer (DGP) on the Churchome app and then answer the questions.

The key also to answering these questions is being *honest* with your response. It's like free therapy! I've been answering these over and over for the past three years now.

And every time I answered, I've learned to believe God for a different response or to "show me" where I am in my "growth sprout."

So, trust the process, the question and answer forum, and the Holy Spirit will do the rest and show you where you are in your growth sprout and if you are *growing*.

If you've been on the Churchome app since 2018 and beyond, then you know who I am... My signature is eyes, heart, praying hands and an upside down smile.

Final Word

No matter what happens in this life, the show must go on... "So, *go* ye into all the world, and preach" (Mark 16:15, NKJV).

Contact Info

Email address: **northwestpca@hotmail.com**

More of my stories can be found on my Facebook page: Karen Hyles.

About the Author

I'm just a church member who likes to write. And I'm so grateful that I got to share my testimony and re-tell the story of Jesus. I gave my heart to Jesus Christ and received the gift of forgiveness. And I love dancing and sipping on my *tea* or grande chai tea latte from Starbucks.

Love ya, church!